B.C.—
BUT THERIOUSLY
FOLKTH...

by
Johnny Hart

FAWCETT GOLD MEDAL • NEW YORK

B.C.—BUT THERIOUSLY FOLKTH ...

A Fawcett Gold Medal Book
Published by Ballantine Books
Copyright © 1975, 1976 Field Enterprises, Inc.
Copyright © 1982 Field Enterprises, Inc.

ISBN 0-449-13197-1

Manufactured in the United States of America

First Ballantine Books Edition: August 1982
Second Printing: March 1987

11-24

11-25

11.26

11-29

12-1

guarantee

a document that expires on the same day as your engine-mounts.

12·2

hart

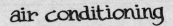

air conditioning

WILEY'S DICTIONARY

12.3

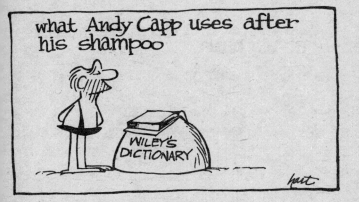

what Andy Capp uses after his shampoo

WILEY'S DICTIONARY

de·part´

de white line down de middle
of de hair

hart

12-5

12-20

12-23

IS THAT THE SAME AS
A FELT TIP FRIEND?

1·3

1-6

RELAX, BIMBO, IT'S FOR THE SPIDER.

1-9

1.13

1·28

2.2

2-3

2.4

2.9

2-13

2-16

* See UNITED NATIONS

2·18

2·24

hart

2 28

3-3

3.4

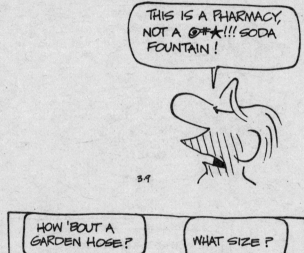

3.9

3-12

3-19

4-19

4-22

EXCUSE ME,
SIR,....

4·2A

hart

4-27

5·5

5-13

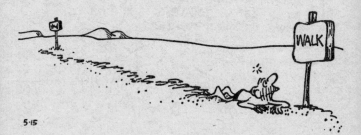

5-15

5-17

5.19

5·21

THANK GOODNESS THE EARTH IS LUMPY.....

5·22

.. OR I'D BE TREADING DIRT ALL DAY.

ANIMALS CRAVING AFFECTION SHOULD
APPROACH THEIR ADVERSARIES IN
THE SUBMISSIVE POSITION.

5·24

BATTER-UP

the traditional cry of
a desperate baker.

B.C.

JOHNNY HART